EXPLORING
BUSINESS
AND
ECONOMICS

EXPLORING
BUSINESS
AND
ECONOMICS

Investing Your Money

Fred Barbash

Chelsea House Publishers

Philadelphia

Frontis: Traders work on the floor of the New York Stock Exchange minutes before the closing bell on Tuesday, March 20, 2001, when lower-than-expected interest rate cuts caused prices to fall, leaving the Dow Jones Industrial Average at its lowest level in two years.

CHELSEA HOUSE PUBLISHERS

EDITOR-IN-CHIEF Sally Cheney
DIRECTOR OF PRODUCTION Kim Shinners
PRODUCTION MANAGER Pamela Loos
ART DIRECTOR Sara Davis

Choptank Syndicate/Chestnut Productions

EDITORIAL Norman Macht and Mary Hull
PRODUCTION Lisa Hochstein
PICTURE RESEARCH Norman Macht

http://www.chelseahouse.com

First Printing

1 3 5 7 9 8 6 4 2

Library of Congress Cataloging-in-Publication Data

Barbash, Fred.
    Investing your money / Fred Barbash.
    p. cm. — (Exploring business and economics)
    ISBN 0-7910-6643-6 (alk. paper)
1. Investments. 2. Finance, Personal. I. Title. II. Series.
HG4521.B3468 2001
332.6—dc21   2001042513

Table of Contents

It costs more to buy an orange in a supermarket today than it did 20 years ago. That's because the cost of growing, harvesting, and shipping oranges has gone up over time. When the prices of things go up, and they cost more money than they used to, that's called inflation.

The Incredible Shrinking Dollar

Any book about investing must begin with the incredible shrinking dollar. If you had plunked a dollar into a piggy bank in 1960 and removed it in the year 2000, you would have been shocked to find that it was worth only 20 cents. A purchase that cost you a dollar in 1960 would have cost you more than $5.00 by 2000.

Comic books used to cost 10 cents; now they cost as much as $3.00. A bottle of soda was a nickel. Today it might be 50 cents or more. In 1970 the cheapest new car on the market was the Volkswagen Beetle, at $2,300. In 2000, a new Beetle went for about $17,000, and the average cost of new cars was $22,000.

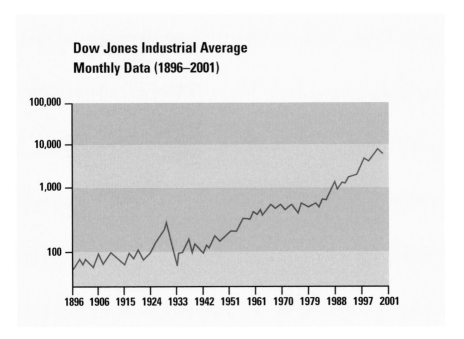

**Dow Jones Industrial Average
Monthly Data (1896–2001)**

This is a chart of the Dow Jones Industrial Average, an indicator of the stock market. It shows that over the long term, people who invested their savings in stocks have seen their money grow in value more than the rate of inflation.

This process of steadily rising prices is called **inflation.** Another way to put it is that your money loses value. It buys less as time goes by. Even getting paid for a job doesn't necessarily mean you will keep up with inflation. A hundred years ago a worker in a factory might earn $500 a year, and be able to support a family. Today that seems hard to believe; $500 a week is hardly enough for even one person to live on. Someone earning $20,000 a year in 1960 would need to earn $100,000 a year in 2000 just to stay even with inflation.

Saving money is a good idea. It's better than spending it on things you don't need. But if saving is all you're doing, you'll lose money. If the future resembles the past at all, the more you save, the less you will have. Because of the ever-rising cost of living, a dollar that just sits in a box or a bank in your room will lose value.

This is why so many people invest their savings. The reason for investing is to make those dollars work for you. Investing is based on the simple fact that people will pay you to use your money. Banks will pay. Governments will pay. Companies will pay. How much they will pay changes all the time and depends on many factors. When you make your dollars available to banks or companies, your money begins working for you. It may earn income and grow in value as a result of your investing. This will be discussed further in Chapter Two, Basic Principles.

Some sacrifice is necessary if you want to be a successful investor. Investing your money is like planting a seed. It takes time for it to grow. If you try to pull it out too soon, you may lose it, like an unripe ear of corn or a green tomato. Just as there is a risk in growing crops that bad weather or plant diseases will ruin them, there is always some risk in investing. If you're not careful about deciding who uses your money and what they do with it, you could lose some or all of it.

Successful investing does not require genius. Millions of people do it. It takes an ability to think about the future, not

Time Is on Your Side

When you're young, it's hard to think about the future. The next weekend, the next movie or ballgame, even the end of the school day may seem a long time away. Waiting for Christmas or next summer seems to take forever. But the sooner you plant your first investment seeds, the greater your reward will grow.

just about what you want to spend your money on today or next week. It helps to have a plan when you start, and to stick to it.

How do people obtain money to invest? They do it by not spending it. They don't spend everything they earn. They don't spend when they don't need to spend. Instead, they put a little aside from each paycheck, sometimes having a a certain amount of money automatically deducted from their account and invested automatically. That way, they don't notice that the money isn't there to spend.

You can begin by not spending all your allowance, or all the money you receive from doing chores or from gifts. Train yourself to always put aside part of whatever money comes into your hands before you buy anything. Pay yourself first. It's a habit that will reward you through-out your life.

Figuring out where to invest money is not difficult. On the other hand, managing your money so that there's some left over to invest can be challenging.

Your goal may be to reach financial independence—to make your money "work" for you. This usually takes many years. Some people succeed so well, they have enough money to harvest in the form of income when they stop working. Sometimes they reach that success early enough in life so they can stop working before the usual retirement age of 65. Others wait until they are 65 or older to leave their jobs, and use the money they've earned and saved to enjoy an easier life.

You may have grandparents, great grandparents, or family friends who have reached that time of their lives. They may travel or play golf or just take it easy, spending their time doing things they enjoy, like gardening and reading. It might be helpful for you to ask them what kind of **retirement**

People have different goals for investing, but for most, it is to have more income and financial security when their working days are over. Today's retirees have more money to travel and enjoy hobbies, sports, and the activities they didn't have time for when they were working and raising families.

plan they have. What did they do with their money while they were working to enable them to live as they do today? How did they invest their savings to help plan for the future?

Like Columbus, who set out looking for Asia but instead reached the Americas, not everyone reaches the goals they set for themselves. Health is a big factor in people's lives. Poor health or a crippling accident can affect one's future even more than successful managing of money. These things are often unpredictable.

You can also learn from people who did not save or invest their money wisely and failed to achieve financial security. Some people who became young millionaires in the booming **stock market** of 1998–99 lost it all when the same technology **stocks** that had made them rich collapsed in the next two years. These were often rags to riches to rags stories. Some of it was due to greed, some to ignorance of the stock market and the basic rules of investing, and some was due to self-proclaimed experts who gave investors bad or misleading advice.

One young executive left his job with $700,000 of **capital** (money). He intended to take a few years off from working to spend more time with his young family. He knew nothing about investing and the stock market. When he met some investment managers who appeared to be experts, he told them he did not want to take a lot of risks and chance losing his money. He then let the managers invest his money for him. At first they made more money for him in very risky investments. But within two years they had lost almost all his money. He was left with only about $400.

Another man lost most of his money in the same way just when he needed it for a child's college tuition. These are not unusual stories. There were many people in their twenties and thirties working for new Internet companies and software giants such as Microsoft who became suddenly wealthy when the stocks they owned in their companies went way up. They became just as suddenly broke when those same stocks went down. Other people invested in those stocks believing that they would go up forever.

Figuring out how to invest your money is challenging. But managing your money so you have some to invest comes first. There is a difference between having the ability to make money and knowing how to manage it once you've made it. Big earners may be big spenders, always over their heads in debt. Misers—people who can't bring themselves to spend any money on anything—are just as unsuccessful at managing money. The key is to find a balance between spending and saving that gives you both a satisfying and financially secure life.

There are many kinds of risk in life. Harry Houdini, an escape artist in the 1920s, often risked his life to demonstrate that he could free himself after being handcuffed, chained in a crate, and thrown into the water. When people invest in the stock market, they risk their money. The risk of losing in either case is always present.

Basic Principles

Think about a NASCAR driver. The faster he goes, the greater his chance of winning the race. But the faster he goes, the greater also is his chance of crashing. Somewhere in between, the good driver finds the right balance of speed and risk.

The same is true when investing money. It's all about balance.

When you invest money, it takes on another name: it's called **principal.** Investing means giving up the use of that principal for a period of time to give it a chance to grow in value. The amount of money it earns for you is called your **rate of return.** If you invest $100 for a year and your investment is worth $108 at the end of that year, your rate of return is eight percent.

You now have $108 to invest instead of merely $100. If you invest the $108 for a year with a rate of return of eight percent, you then have $116.64. An average rate of return of eight percent a year for 50 years will turn your $100 investment into $4,960.16. The term used to describe this annual addition to your initial investment is **compounding.** When you reinvest earnings on a regular basis so that the principal continues to grow, you are making money "work" for you. That's how $1,000 can become $50,000 and $10,000 becomes $500,000. People who make an investment plan and stick to it can become wealthy even if they never earn a big salary. It takes patience and time, but it works.

Nobody can guarantee an eight percent return every year or even an average of eight percent over any time period. Returns from investing vary a lot. But eight percent is less than the annual growth rate of the stock market for the past 50 years, so it's not unrealistic.

Of course, life is full of all kinds of risks, and investing, too, can be risky. What do we mean by risk? A risk is a chance of losing something. People who smoke risk the

Warren Buffet

Warren Buffet, the chairman of Berkshire Hathaway Corporation, is one of the richest people in the world and probably the most famous investor of our times. His specialty is buying traditional companies that make ordinary products such as candy, bricks, and shoes, when they are cheap, and then helping them grow. Following the rule of diversifying, his company owns more than 50 different businesses of all kinds. Millions of investors have made a lot of money by investing in his company.

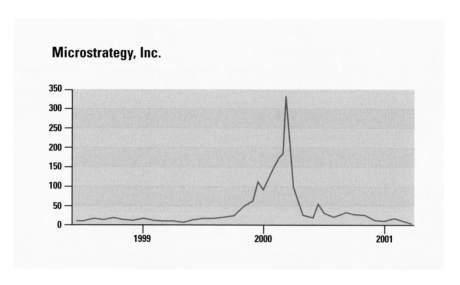

Microstrategy, Inc.

It took about two years for the price of Microstrategy, Inc. to go from $3 a share to over $300 and back down to $3 in 2001. Of the 1,262 companies that went public between 1998 and 2000, few were successful. One in eight fell to under $1 a share.

loss of their health. Someone driving 85 miles an hour on a highway with a 55 speed limit takes several risks: their speeding may cause an accident; it may endanger someone else's life; they may get a ticket from a police officer.

A prudent person who takes a risk measures it against the possible reward. In the case of the smoker the reward is the immediate feeling of smoking the cigarette. The speeding driver may get where he is going a few minutes sooner. Each person must ask himself: is the possible reward worth the risk I'm taking?

There are two ways to measure risk: how much might I lose, and what is the chance of my losing? These are important questions for investors to think about before they risk their money.

You have low-risk friends to whom you would lend money, confident that they will pay you back when they promise. On the other hand, you probably have friends you would never expect to pay you back. These could be called your seriously high-risk friends. In the middle of these two extremes you probably have medium-risk friends, who might or might not repay you. Figuring the chances of getting paid back, not by friends but by different investments, is what investors do when they decide how much risk they want to take.

When investors think about the chances of losing their money, they ask themselves: "What are my chances of getting my money back? If I don't get the money back, how much will I suffer? Can I afford to lose it all? If not, is there a different, safer investment?"

Deciding how to invest your money requires some tough choices and self-control. The most tempting investments, the ones promising the largest returns, may also be the riskiest. If you choose the safest investments, you're likely to make less of a profit.

When it comes to risks and returns, the world of investing is a world of extremes. When investors lend money to the United States government, by purchasing a **bond,** a note issued by someone borrowing money, they take little risk because the government has always paid its debts. But they get only a modest return on the investment. When investors buy stock in a new software company, they could double their money. On the other hand, the company might go out of business and they could lose it all.

The range of risk is one of the reasons many investors spread their money among different types of investments. If they put all they had into new software companies, for example, they could lose everything they invested and be broke when they retired. By putting some money in low-risk investments, a portion in medium risks, and some in

Great fortunes were made by the builders of the first railroads to cross the United States linking the east and west coasts.

high-risk investments, investors protect themselves. They also stand a better chance of getting a high return on their total investments.

So what is the best way for you to begin? First of all, you should not invest any money you're saving up to buy something. Your investments should not be touched for many years to give them a chance to grow. If you expect to spend the money in a few months or even a year, let it stay in your savings account.

If you have some extra money you'd like to use to start investing, perhaps the best way to begin is by thinking about the products you like and use. What brands of cereals, sodas, or cookies do you like? Do you go to McDonald's? Do you buy clothes or toys at Wal-Mart?

Many people like to invest in companies whose products they use. If you like General Mills fruit roll-ups or cereals, for example, and you think the company's value is likely to increase, you might consider buying a share of their stock.

Does your family use Sara Lee or French's products? Companies such as Pepsico, Coca-Cola, Kellogg, General Mills, McDonald's, Wal-Mart, Sara Lee and French's are all publicly owned. **Shares** of stock in these companies are actively traded. All are regarded as well-managed companies with growth potential.

If you own even one share of stock in any of them, you are a part owner of that company. Every time you use their products or go into one of their stores, you'll know that you're helping your own business grow. You'll be able to look in the newspaper and see what price your stock traded at the day before. You'll receive reports from the company telling you about new products or new stores, and how well they're doing. You'll have a firsthand look at how businesses operate in the national and world economy.

Later, as you begin to work and have more money to invest, you may think about investing in a wider variety of stocks. Then a **mutual fund** may be a good way for you to go. We'll explain mutual funds in Chapter Five.

As your life changes when you're older and you find you might need some of your investment money for expenses, the rules of investing change. A parent who's going to need $50,000 for college tuition in two years should be careful to make sure that the money will be available by placing at least that amount in something really safe. A young person who sees no need to tap into investments for 30 years can obviously take greater chances.

The other reason to avoid "putting all your eggs in one basket" is that most investments do well in some years and badly in others. The only thing you can be sure of is that nobody can predict the future. By making sure money is spread out, the investor stands a greater chance of obtaining continuous growth rather than going through long periods of no growth at all or even losses.

Diversifying—putting your money in different kinds of investments, is probably the single most important rule of investing. It's the best protection against disaster and may be the best route to the highest rate of return. **Asset allocation** is the process of deciding how much of your money to place in various types of investments according to your goals, age, and financial situation. Professional financial advisers can help with this—for a fee. Some investors, particularly wealthy investors, turn to financial advisers and money managers to invest for them.

As the stories in this chapter demonstrate, the final responsibility for what happens to your money will be yours. How you spend it, how much you save, and how you invest it will be up to you. How much risk you are willing to take is for you to decide. Some people are more comfortable with risk than others. You also have to judge if the advice someone is giving you is suitable for you.

Suppose someone told you how exciting it would be to ride your bicycle over a cliff. What a thrill to fly through the air. Would you do it? Or would you say, "That's not for me. I don't want to take the risk of getting hurt or killed. It's not worth it." But what if they assured you it was safe, the drop was only 10 feet, and other people had done it? "I'm an expert in bike riding," they tell you. "I know what I'm talking about." Would you still say no?

That's the kind of advice and assurances that people hear every day from other investors and some professionals in the investment business. Sometimes it's good advice, sometimes it isn't. It's up to each person to listen and judge the advice and the person who is giving it. It's important to be comfortable with the advisor and the advice, to feel right about it, to know that what you're being told fits the way you feel about your money.

There's an old saying in the stock market about people who own a lot of stocks and are worried about them going down in value: "Sell to the sleeping point." It means such a person should sell as much stock as it takes for them to be able to sleep at night without worrying about losing their money.

Some people never worry about money. Their attitude is, "Easy come, easy go. If I lose all my money, I'll just work and make some more." Those people don't mind taking chances and risks to make a big profit or lose everything they have. Some legendary investors of the past became rich and poor and rich again and poor again many times during their eventful lives.

That's one extreme. At the other end, some people are so worried about losing a nickel, they don't even trust the banks, and wouldn't lend the United States government a dime.

Somewhere in between, each person must find their own comfort level. Once you've found yours, guard it. Don't let anyone lure you away from it, no matter what riches they dangle in front of you.

The Financial Machine

The investment industry has created a worldwide system for bringing together those in need of money with those who have money to invest. Those in need of money include startup businesses, small businesses, huge corporations, county, state, and national governments, banks, and families trying to buy houses or send children to college. The school down the street, the factory across town, the bridge across the river, the very sidewalks you walk on, and the highways you drive on have been bought and paid for through this system. So has much of the technological and scientific innovation of our modern era.

There are many stories of people with great ideas who started businesses in garages, basements, or, more recently, in college dorm rooms. But without a way to raise the capital they need to build a business, these ideas can only remain ideas. That capital may come from investors, ranging from the teenager investing his savings to giant corporation pension funds investing the retirement money of millions of employees.

There are a few basic ways most commonly used to raise the needed capital. A company may sell shares of the business—called common stock. They may borrow the money by selling notes called bonds. Banks sell **Certificates of Deposit (CDs)** to investors in order to finance bank lending activity.

It is important that people have confidence in the honesty of the system. Without laws and regulations to protect investors, people would not trust anyone with their hard-earned money. They would hide it under mattresses or bury it in the backyard. Some people who don't trust banks or anyone else do just that. Nobody benefits from that.

In some countries nobody knows who owns the buildings or land. Nobody has a clear legal title to their property, so they can't borrow any money on it. That means they are not likely to do anything to improve it. That's one reason farmers in poor countries are stuck in poverty and it is almost impossible for anyone to raise the money to build up a business.

Probably the single most important legal underpinning in our society is the **contract.** A contract is an agreement, enforceable in a court of law, that binds one party to do something with or for another.

It's like a promise, except that it's usually written down. When you promise to mow the lawn or run an errand for

After five years of rising stock prices, the market suddenly crashed on October 24, 1929, leading to the Great Depression. During the next four years, stock prices lost 80 percent of their value. Bank failures wiped out the savings of millions of people.

someone, and you don't do it, you've broken your promise—your contract. If you borrow something and promise to return it, and don't, you've broken a contract. If someone offers to pay you a dollar to do a job, then refuses to pay you, that's a broken contract. None of them were written down, but they were spoken contracts. If someone's word—or written promise—isn't good, you don't want to do business with that person.

Without enforceable contracts, nobody would trust anyone else with their money. The financial system would grind to a halt. Imagine sending your money to a bunch of strangers, such as investment managers you don't know, without some assurance of being able to take them to court if the strangers turned out to be fakes. Imagine buying a company's bond—lending them money—if that bond or note was a meaningless piece of paper rather than a contract that can be enforced. In countries without court systems to enforce contracts, there is no financial system, and very little development can take place.

In the United States, the **Securities and Exchange Commission (SEC)** regulates the investment industry. There are laws to protect investors against fraud—false statements about a company's profits, for example, or salesmen peddling phony stocks. The government also regulates the activities of banks, and insures bank accounts so you won't lose all your money if the bank suddenly goes out of business.

How many people would feel comfortable investing in a company if its officers could lie about profits and get away with it? How many people would feel comfortable putting money in a bank if the bank could do anything it pleased with the money? Insurance programs sponsored by the government or investment industry add to the comfort of investors. The **Federal Deposit Insurance Corporation**

Keeping Up with the Financial News

The Wall Street Journal is the most famous financial newspaper in the United States. *Money* magazine and *SmartMoney* magazine are consumer-oriented financial weeklies. The CNBC network provides constant TV coverage of the stock market. *Wall Street Week* provides a weekly discussion of the markets on public television. On National Public Radio, the program "Marketplace" focuses on news related to investing.

(FDIC), for example, insures bank deposits, including interest-paying certificates of deposit, up to $100,000. The **Securities Investor Protection Corporation (SIPC)** assures investors that if a brokerage firm runs off with all their money, they'll be repaid. That doesn't protect you against losing investments, just against someone stealing your money.

The financial services industry is the force that drives the global financial system. It includes brokerage houses, investment banks, mutual fund companies, **stock exchanges,** and banks. It's a multi-trillion dollar business that spans the globe. Most of these companies act as agents (brokers) bringing together those who need money with those who have it to invest.

The majority of these companies, including the **New York Stock Exchange (NYSE),** are headquartered in the financial district of New York City, on or near Wall Street. That's the reason people sometimes refer to Wall Street as if it was a person who expressed their emotions for all the world to hear: "Wall Street liked today's news;" "Wall Street was unhappy;" or "Wall Street got a big surprise."

Individual investors cannot walk onto the floor of the New York Stock Exchange and buy shares of stock. There are too many of them. It would be a constant riot. Brokers, acting as middlemen, do it for them. Nor can a company simply go door to door in neighborhoods borrowing little bits of money until it has collected $1 billion. It would use up all its time raising money and would never raise enough. Companies specializing in bonds do this for them.

Consider the purchase of shares of **common stock.** Because it can be done in minutes by anyone sitting at a computer terminal, it seems simple. But the order travels first to a brokerage, then perhaps to a trading company,

The New York Stock Exchange at the end of the day. The floor around the trading posts is littered with discarded notes of the day's activity. Although a membership in the exchange is called a seat, you can see that there is no place to sit while the exchange is open for trading.

then perhaps to a stock exchange, before working its way back with a message that says the stock has been bought.

The financial services industry has given the same lone investor global reach. A hundred years ago, the average American's money transactions were confined to a neighborhood, perhaps a county. Today the ordinary person routinely invests in securities around the world or in the shares of foreign companies sold on American exchanges. Foreigners and foreign governments invest in American companies and buy United States government bonds. The individual investor, not just big corporations, is now multinational.

This is why foreign stock markets react instantly to what happens in the American market. "When the United States sneezes," the saying goes, "the world catches a cold." This opportunity to invest almost anywhere in the world arises from the financial system's ability to bring together those who need money with those who have it, no matter where they all live. Should this system break down anywhere along the line, the wheels of world finance would stop turning.

Confidence in the financial system requires a free press: newspapers, magazines, television, and Internet sources of news uncontrolled by the government or by the financial services industry. In a 17th century society where only a few wealthy aristocrats had money to invest, perhaps the press played no role. Information about the economy, individual companies, and markets could be spread by personal contacts. But in modern-day America, there are tens of millions of investors. The mass media is the only way to distribute information quickly among so many people, not only information about specific companies and investments, but also about the general economic climate.

The best investors are the best informed. No one can become a good investor by concentrating only on techniques of investing. Keeping up to date on the world around them is just as important.

Let's talk about matchmaking again. When a company needs money to grow, it can borrow the money or it can

Bull Market or Bear Market?

A bull market is the term used to describe a strong stock market, with generally rising prices. It can last a few months or many years. When the market has been going down for several months, it is called a bear market.

Foreign stock markets, like this one in Kuwait, react to what happens in American stock exchanges. This is because the world is tied together through global trade.

issue common stock to raise the money. A company issuing stock is selling part of the business to investors. Stocks or shares are also called **equities.** It sells the shares at a certain price in an **initial public offering (IPO)** and receives the funds for its use. People who buy the shares are then free to sell them to other investors in the "secondary market" or "aftermarket." The money this time goes from investor to investor. Nothing goes to the company. The stock market everyone talks about is a secondary market.

There are no guarantees in the stock market. You can make a lot of money and lose a lot. Sometimes people become frightened when stock prices go down, and they are panicked into selling their stocks. When the price of their stock is going up, they feel very smart. They expect it to go up forever and can't imagine that it will ever go back down again. These emotions affect their decisions. There is an old rule in the stock market: the way to become rich is to buy when prices are low and sell when they are high. But most people do just the opposite. They are so worried when all the news is bad and stocks are down in price, they are afraid to invest. And when all the news is good and stock prices are soaring, they think the prices will go up forever and they would feel foolish to sell. It's their own emotions that are working against them. One result is that the stock market goes up and down, sometimes way up or way down in a short time.

The stock market is not a place. It's an activity—the buying and selling of the stocks of different companies. When someone says they are in the stock market, they're really saying that they invest in stocks. When someone says, "How did the market do today?" they're trying to find out if stock prices went up or down in the day's trading. In 2000 there were about 7,000 publicly traded companies on the stock market.

Most stock trading takes place through exchanges, marketplaces for the buying and selling of shares. The world's oldest continuously operating stock exchange is the London Stock Exchange in the United Kingdom. It got started in Jonathan's Coffee House, where brokers traded shares of the Muscovy Company, founded in 1553. In 1760, they changed the name of the coffee house to the Stock Exchange.

The newest large exchange, called the North American Securities Dealers Automated Quotation system (NASDAQ), was established in 1968 and is entirely computer-driven. The Philadelphia Stock Exchange, established in 1790, is the oldest in America. The New York Stock Exchange (NYSE), the largest, was established in 1817.

The NYSE still uses floor traders who gather around trading posts to conduct auctions that set the prices of stocks. (Until 2000 stock prices were quoted exclusively in fractions such as $10^1/8$, $10^3/16$, $10^1/2$, and so forth. The practice originated from silver and gold coins that could be broken into eight pieces. Starting in 2000, the major exchanges began converting to decimals so that $10^1/2$ would become \$10.50.) In recent years smaller market-places have emerged, using the latest technology to conduct stock trading.

Many people who do online trading over the Internet think they're actually communicating directly with a stock exchange. They aren't. Investors place orders with brokers, either over the Internet or on the phone. For a fee, the brokers relay the orders to the exchange or to a trading company with access to the exchange.

Through the exchange, the price at which buyers are willing to buy the stock is compared with the price at which sellers are willing to sell it. It's an auction. If a lot of people want to buy a particular stock, sellers will ask more and the price will go up. If a lot of people would rather sell than buy, they'll drive the price downward.

What if the sell price and the buy price never really match? What happens if someone wants to sell but nobody in the world wants to buy the stock on that day? To avoid this problem, the stock exchange has people called "market makers" who will buy or sell such stocks at the going price. This provides **liquidity**—the ability to quickly and easily turn an investment into cash—to the market. Without the confidence that an investment can be easily turned into cash when you need it, fewer people would invest in stocks.

Watching the market has become a national pastime, with the ups and downs of the three main market indexes featured as regularly as the weather each day in all news reports. If you turn on the news, you'll hear the temperature, the latest sports scores, and always the latest on the Dow Jones Industrial Average, the NASDAQ Composite, and the Standard and Poor's Index of 500 stocks (S&P 500). Each is a collection of stocks meant to represent a portion of the market. They indicate the overall direction of prices. For some investors, these indexes serve as benchmarks with which they can compare their own gains and losses each year. Watching the stock market, clicking a mouse, dialing the phone, placing an order—this is the easiest part of stock trading. Choosing the right investment for each individual is the challenge.

The money to build bridges like the Golden Gate in San Francisco, and tunnels and turnpikes, is often borrowed from the public through the sale of bonds. Toll revenues may be used to pay the interest and repay the loan.

Stocks, Bonds, Futures, and Options

When considering an investment, investors look for a good return on the money invested. They look for it, but they don't always get it. Their hopes are not always rewarded. Their plans, no matter how carefully they have made them, don't always turn out as they expected. But many times the seeds they have planted do grow into very prosperous and wealthy flowers. This can happen because the value of their stocks has grown, the company has shared some of its profits with the investor in the form of **dividends,** or both.

Appreciation, or growth of a stock's price, is dependent on the demand for the stock: whether or not others are willing to

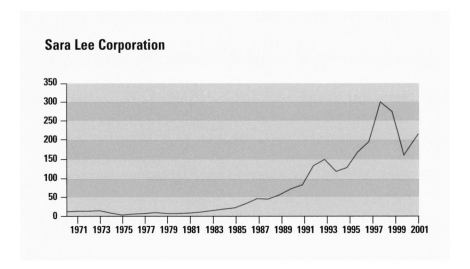

Sara Lee Corporation

Sara Lee Corporation is an example of a company that has grown steadily over the past 20 years. Although all stocks go up and down in price, a growth stock's value will usually follow a generally rising path.

purchase it at a price higher than you paid. Demand depends on how well the company's profits grow. Companies publicly report their earnings—if they have any—every three months. Serious investors keep track of these reports to see how the company is doing. But it's important to remember that companies are reporting the past, what they have already done. The demand for a stock is based more on its future, which of course remains unknown. Investors who act only on the basis of today's news and reports of what has already happened are looking in the wrong direction—backward instead of ahead.

The price of a stock says nothing about how expensive it is. What matters is the price compared to the earnings of the company represented by the stock. A stock priced at $100 a share with terrific profits may be a bargain compared to a $20 stock in a company that is losing money. Professionals speak of a stock as overpriced when the price per share seems too high in relation to present or expected future profits.

Investors believe that if they've bought the stock of a company that remains profitable, they should give it a chance and hold it for many years. They are long-term investors. People who buy and sell stocks frequently, holding them for very short periods, are called **speculators,** or traders, rather than investors. Investors come out ahead in the long run.

Many profitable companies pay dividends, distributing a share of profits to stockholders. Only well established profitable companies can even think about paying dividends. Newer companies or companies heavily involved in research and development reinvest all their profits back into the company.

How do dividends work? Suppose the profit to be distributed in a particular year is $2 million. Suppose there are a million shares outstanding—owned by investors. When a company pays out the dividend, each share would receive

Certificates of Deposit

Bonds are a fixed income investment because the rate of return is fixed at the time of purchase. A Certificate of Deposit (CD) issued by a bank is also a fixed income investment. As with a bond, the investor is lending money, this time to the bank, in exchange for a stream of payments. An advantage of CDs is that the Federal Deposit Insurance Corporation guarantees them. A disadvantage is that if you try to obtain your money before the maturity date, you may pay a penalty. Another disadvantage is that you can not ordinarily sell CDs.

$2.00. An investor who owned 100 shares would receive $200 in dividends.

Two dollars doesn't sound like much. How much it really is depends on what you paid for the stock, how long you hold the stock, how frequently it pays a dividend, and whether or not the dividend increases regularly. It can add up nicely.

If the stock cost $40 and pays $2 in dividends per year, that's a strong dividend yield of 5 percent. Suppose the company continued paying those two dollars every year. In 10 years the stockholder would accumulate $20 of income from the $40 investment. That's 50 percent of the price of the stock without selling the stock. Reinvesting the dividend every year will produce even more growth. If the dividend increased every year and the stockholder held onto the stock for a long time, it would eventually pay for itself—and then some.

Companies paying dividends are sometimes described as "income stocks" because investors buy them to produce income, perhaps in retirement when they no longer have a job. Stocks bought primarily with price appreciation in mind

Interest Rates

The level of interest rates is probably the single most important influence on financial markets and on the cost of consumer borrowing. The Federal Reserve Board, a U.S. government agency, is the most important influence on interest rates. It can force them up or down by varying the cost of lending government funds to large borrowers such as banks, or by varying the supply of dollars. Alan Greenspan became a household name in the 1990s as the Chairman of the Federal Reserve Board.

are growth stocks. Some stocks grow and pay dividends, too, and are called "growth and income stocks."

No stock guarantees either growth or income forever. Industries change as they grow older. New inventions may put the makers of old equipment out of business. Automobiles replaced horse-drawn carriages. Electricity replaced whale oil and kerosene lamps. Computers replaced typewriters. Some of the best investments of the past no longer exist today. Nobody knows what the next revolutionary inventions may be. Any stock can become a loser.

Historically, the stock market has been hit by both manias and panics. Manias occur when enthusiastic investors overestimate the potential for a company's growth and bid up prices too high, producing a "bubble." This occurred in 1998 and 1999 with the stocks of technology companies, particularly the so-called "dot coms" of the Internet world. When the latest greatest thing turns out not to be so great, investors dump the stocks quickly, often in a panic, causing prices to drop quickly. Sometimes the stocks of perfectly good companies get dragged down in the panic.

The terms "stocks and bonds" often go together. They are the two most common investments in the world and the greatest source of money for big business and government. While the stock market attracts more attention, bonds attract far more money.

A bond is an agreement to borrow a specific amount of money at a stated cost, or interest rate, for a limited period of time. When you purchase a bond, you are lending money to a company or government.

If you've ever borrowed money from a friend and written an "IOU" promising to pay it back, you've given something like a bond. Unlike stocks, bonds do not give the investor any ownership in the business. Bondholders do not enjoy

Governments have been borrowing money by selling bonds for thousands of years. A bond is an IOU that promises to repay the amount of the loan on a stated date, and to pay interest on the loan in the meantime. This U.S. savings bond, featuring Albert Einstein, was introduced in 1998.

the benefits of a company's growth. But also unlike stocks, bonds promise a steady, fixed income to the bondholder, which is why they are called fixed income investments.

The issuer of a bond pays interest (a fee for the use of the money) to the purchaser of the bond. The cost of money changes constantly as interest rates rise and fall. One day it might cost 5 cents to borrow a dollar (5 percent) for a year. The next day it might cost 5.1 cents (5.1 percent). The next year it might cost 6 cents. The year after that it might shoot down to 4 cents per dollar borrowed.

The law of supply and demand is again at work. When money is plentiful, the cost of borrowing tends to decline. When money is scarce, the cost tends to increase. The strength of the bond issuer is equally important. A strong company that is likely to pay the interest and repay the principal on time can borrow money more cheaply than a shaky company. Companies have credit ratings, as do individuals. The higher the rating, the safer the investment, and the interest rate paid to the lender will be lower. A bond with a low or risky rating will have to pay a higher interest rate to borrow money.

American humorist Will Rogers had that in mind when he said, "The return of my money is more important to me than the return on my money."

The United States government issues the safest bonds. The government borrows huge amounts of money—trillions of dollars—because it doesn't collect enough money in taxes to pay for its vast operations. Most of the national debt is owed to bond investors, including young people who have savings bonds. The United States government has never failed to pay the interest and the principal to a borrower. Being so safe, government bonds tend to pay lower interest rates than corporate bonds. The simplest way to buy a government bond is to buy a new issue online directly from the Department of the Treasury.

City and state governments also issue bonds—called Municipals or "Munis" for short—to finance the construction of bridges, schools, roads, highways, and other public works projects. Wealthy investors, especially, like Munis because they don't have to pay federal income tax on the interest paid. Many toll bridges and highways are built by selling bonds, and the interest is paid from the tolls that are collected.

In addition to stocks and bonds, there are other specialized types of investments. Some people collect rare stamps, old coins, gold, artworks, baseball cards, autographs, or antiques of all kinds. But for most people, stocks and bonds are the best kinds of seeds to plant to make their money grow.

Most bonds offer two different ways to make (or lose) money: holding the bond until it comes due, or "matures," or selling it before the maturity date—the date when the principal is paid back—in the bond market.

Bond prices go up or down as interest rates fluctuate. Suppose you buy a $1,000 Treasury bond paying 6 percent interest. That's a guaranteed income of $60 a year. If interest rates are lower a year later, and interest payments on new Treasury bonds fall to 5 percent, your 6 percent bond will be in demand. You may be able to sell your $1,000 bond for more than you paid for it because it provides $60 a year in income, while new bonds are only paying $50 a year. If interest rates go up, your bond may go down in price. Changes in bond prices should not matter much if you hold a bond to maturity. The interest paid by a bond (its yield) does matter. If the cost of living rises faster than the interest rate of a bond, you fall behind.

The bond market is much more difficult to navigate for an individual investor than the stock market. There's no centralized listing of all bond prices. Bonds, corporate and government, come in many different flavors, making it difficult to compare bond prices.

People highly trained in bond trading with the proper resources sometimes make large profits or incur large losses. Untrained individuals interested in profiting from bond trading tend to purchase bond mutual funds.

Sometime in your life, you may hear that someone is trading in soybean **futures** or corn futures or wheat futures, ordering 5,000 or 10,000 bushels at a time. You may picture a living room full of soybeans or a railroad freight pulling up in your neighborhood filled with corn or potatoes. Don't worry about it. The vast majority of people who trade in these commodities futures are after money, not beans or grains. If you trade in soybean futures, you'll never have to touch a soybean, let alone eat one.

Trading in futures and their close cousins, **options,** involves making a bet, based on an informed guess, that

How many pigs there are in the country is important information for people who trade in futures such as pork bellies, which is where bacon comes from.

something will go up or down in price without actually buying that particular thing.

The following example doesn't happen in real life, but it may help in understanding futures trading. Suppose someone's selling a compact disc by an unknown group. You're not that interested in the music, but you think the group will become very popular soon, resulting in a doubling of the price of its first album. You don't really want to buy the album. You've just got a hunch and see the possibility of selling later for a profit. You pay your friend $10 and promise you'll accept (and then sell) his album within six months. The friend agrees because he needs some money now.

Some people use collectibles as another form of investment. This rare circa 1909 Honus Wagner baseball card sold in 2000 for over $1 million— a record for a baseball card.

Five months pass. The group is a huge hit. Even though you don't yet actually own that album, you are able to sell it to someone else for $20. You paid only $10. You've doubled your money. But what if the group remained unknown and the value of the album plunged to zero? You'd lose the $10 you'd spent on a now worthless album.

This is close to the way futures and options work. They are gambles that the price of something will go up or down—such things as soybeans, pork bellies, wheat, petroleum, gold, silver, stock market indexes, individual stocks, foreign currency, even the weather.

People trade options and futures for two reasons. For some people it may be a form of protection called a hedge. In fact, futures began as a way for farmers to lock in a price on a crop before it was ready for harvest. If the price of the crop was lower when harvest time came around, they were in luck because they had already sold it at a higher price.

The second reason people trade in futures and options is because it is possible to make a lot of money without risking a lot. But, as we discussed earlier, the risk of losing whatever money you did put up is large. If you put up just 10 percent of the total cost of a contract of wheat or corn, for example, and the price goes up 10 percent, you have doubled your money. But if the price goes down 10 percent, you have lost your entire investment.

A futures contract is an obligation to buy, or to sell, a certain quantity of something at a specified time in the future. If you've bought a contract "long," you've agreed to take delivery of that something. If you've bought short, you've agreed to deliver it. You'll most likely never do either. You'll be selling that futures contract long before the specified time. It's the contracts that are really being traded, not the corn and beans themselves.

The four broad classes of commodities are grains and oilseeds, livestock and meat, metals and petroleum, and food and fiber. The first includes corn, oats, wheat, barley, flaxseed, and rice. The second includes cattle, hogs, and pork bellies. Examples of the third class are electricity, copper, gold, gasoline, and propane. The fourth includes cocoa, coffee, cotton, orange juice, and sugar. The Chicago Mercantile Exchange even trades weather futures. They are used by firms, such as gas and electric utilities, that stand to lose money depending on the rise and fall of temperatures.

Options are similar to futures because investors are acquiring the right (the option) to buy or sell something over a specific time period. It could be commodities, stocks, stock indexes, foreign currency, even futures contracts. The most significant difference between options and futures is that

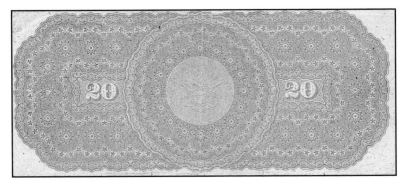

Rare coins and currency are another collector's item and form of investment. This 1866 $20 U.S. gold certificate was recently discovered in New England and its worth has been estimated at over $250,000.

futures contracts obligate the investor to buy or sell. Options contracts merely give you the right to buy or sell. You don't have to do anything. The money making possibility from options trading derives, as it does in futures, from obtaining an interest in something worth many times more than your investment. This increases both your profit potential and risk. The amount you can lose is no more than the cost of the option, but the chance of losing it all is very high.

There are other kinds of investing that are far from the ones we've been talking about. Some people collect rare stamps, old coins, dolls, art works, baseball cards, or antiques of all kinds, because they enjoy collecting them and they believe the objects will increase in value over the years. Many of these investments have a limited supply; there are no more airmail stamps printed upside down, for example, or old Babe Ruth baseball cards, or ancient Roman coins being made. If the demand for these kinds of objects increases, the few available to buy will increase in price.

A roomful of day traders work at ProTrader Securities in Atlanta, Georgia, in 2001. Day trading is a risky practice that gained popularity when the market was rising, among ordinary investors lured by the prospect of quick riches. When the stock market fell, many day traders lost all their money.

Mutual Funds

Investing in the markets—whether stocks or bonds—was once a rich man's game. Trading was expensive, as was the cost of research to find the best investments. Two developments changed everything: the creation of mutual funds and the beginning of Internet-based, or online, investing.

A mutual fund pools the money of thousands, even millions of individuals, and invests it for them. It may invest in almost anything: U.S. stocks, foreign stocks, bonds, precious metals, even other mutual funds. It may invest in one type of **securities,** or many different types. Within stocks, it may choose to specialize in particular industries: health care, technology, oil, or transportation, for example. Some mutual funds invest only in large growth stocks, others in income stocks. Some include both.

When you purchase a mutual fund, you buy shares in that fund. If the stocks or other securities owned by the fund do

Websites That Assist Investors

WWW.MORNINGSTAR.COM—Sponsored by a leading independent research company, this site provides vast amounts of data, clearly explained, with a specialty in mutual funds.

WWW.MOTLEYFOOL.COM—The Motley Fool is famous for its analyses and especially for its amusing tone.

WWW.SEC.GOV—The site run by the United State's government's Securities and Exchange Commission offers information to protect small investors as well as access to reports filed with the SEC by publicly traded companies.

WWW.NASD.COM—The extremely useful homepage of the NASDAQ.

WWW.CBOT.COM—The Chicago Board of Trade website, which includes detailed explanations of futures and options.

WWW.PUBLICDEBT.GOV—All about government bonds, from the United States Department of The Treasury.

WWW.SMARTMONEY.COM—This Dow Jones Company site includes a useful color-coded "map of the market" each day as well as information about companies and articles about the markets.

WWW.BIGCHARTS.COM—This is the best site for obtaining charts showing the movements of stocks and indexes over time.

Some companies own so many different businesses, their name doesn't tell you what they do or make. The Otter Tail Power Company, which began as an electric company, now owns a baseball team as well as plastics, health services, and other manufacturing businesses. As a result, the company changed its name to Otter Tail Corporation.

well, your investment will benefit. If they do poorly, so will you. Unlike stocks, you can't sell mutual fund shares to another investor. Most funds buy and sell their own shares directly with the public. Their prices don't depend on public supply and demand. The shares are priced at the exact value of the fund's investments at the end of each day.

A mutual fund that is always buying in its old shares and selling new ones is called an open end fund. There is no limit to the number of shares it can sell. There is a second kind of mutual fund that is called a closed end fund. That means the fund has a fixed number of shares, and it does not buy them back when you want to sell. A closed end fund's shares are traded like any other stock, its price subject to supply and demand. Sometimes it may sell for less than the actual value of the stocks the fund holds, and sometimes it may sell for more, depending on the demand for the shares.

The first mutual funds appeared in the 1920s but did not gain a mass following until the 1960s. By the 1990s, more mutual funds than stocks were available to investors.

Between 1981 and 2001, the value of equity mutual funds alone soared from $41 billion to $3.7 trillion, a hundredfold increase. In 2001, the total amount invested in all mutual funds was about $7 trillion.

Three advantages of mutual funds account for their great popularity. The investor need not do the time-consuming research necessary to select individual stocks. The fund hires professional managers for that. Funds offer the average investor greater diversity than otherwise available. Only the wealthiest of individuals could possibly buy the number and variety of investments held by a typical mutual fund. A stock mutual fund may own shares of anywhere from 20 to 200 different companies.

Finally, an investor can purchase mutual fund shares for as little as $1,000 or $1,500. If the purchasing is regular, through deductions from a paycheck or bank account, shares can be purchased for even smaller amounts, $50 or $100. It's impossible to open an account at a brokerage firm and buy stocks with so little money.

For all but the wealthiest, mutual funds may be the only way to invest in some things, such as precious metals.

Real estate investment trusts (REITs) are close cousins of mutual funds, offering the investor a share in commercial real estate ventures, such as shopping centers, malls, apartments, and office buildings.

Because of the number and variety of mutual funds, choosing among them has become almost as challenging as choosing stocks. Within each category of fund, hundreds of companies compete for the investing dollar. Many books, magazines, newsletters, and websites exist to help people compare funds. While many people look at a particular fund's return over a long period of time to help make a decision, past performance is no guarantee of future performance. Some mutual funds charge a fee, called a load, to buy their shares. Others, called no-load funds, do not. All of them charge a fee to manage the fund. This cost varies among funds, and is usually deducted from the investor's account.

Mutual fund ownership truly exploded with the arrival in the 1970s of retirement plans such as 401(k) plans and Individual Retirement Accounts (IRAs). These are ways for anyone earning income to save and invest to build a comfortable retirement fund for themselves.

In a 401(k) plan, an employer puts a portion of an employee's paycheck into investments selected by the employee. That portion of the paycheck is not taxed either by the federal or state governments until retirement, when the employee starts to withdraw the money. Neither are the gains from the investments taxed until they are in the employee's hands. The most common choice for investing 401(k) money is mutual funds. Many people also choose to put their money into shares of the company they work for. That kind of investment in a company like Wal-Mart, for example, has made millionaires of some

Some money managers have built successful records over long periods of time. One such "star" is Charles M. "Chuck" Royce, who has been president and chief investment officer of the Royce Funds for more than 25 years.

ordinary employees. By 2001, some 50 million Americans were enrolled in 401(k) plans with assets of $2.3 trillion.

IRAs offer similar advantages with the difference that the investor sets up the account by himself, choosing the particular investments held in it. No employer is involved. With both forms of tax-protected accounts, you lose access to your money for a long period of time. With some exceptions, you can't touch the money until the later years of life, which is why people call them retirement accounts. The idea of helping people plant the seeds early in life to provide for a richer, more secure retirement is relatively new. But it has already proven that it works. It's never too early for anyone earning income to begin such a plan.

The Internet has inspired other new ways of investing. Of special interest to small investors or young people, web-based brokerage accounts permit the purchase of stocks by dollar amount. With dollar-based investing, you order, say, $20 worth of IBM, perhaps every month, and obtain whatever fraction of an IBM share $20 will buy. The two pioneering companies offering this service are BuyAndHold.com and Sharebuilder.com.

In 1989 it was difficult to find a broker who would charge anything less than $200 for a single stock trade. Ten years later, you could do it for $7. What happened? The Internet came along with low-cost online trading of stocks and many other types of investments.

Online trading is deceptively simple. An investor opens an account by sending in a certain amount of money, often about $2,000. He gets an account number and a password to log in. Without further ado, he can begin buying stocks. Online trading seems speedy. But trade execution is no faster than the brokerage's capacity to process orders. Orders to buy and sell wait in line for anywhere from 30 seconds to 30 minutes or longer, depending on market conditions. A price can change significantly during this lag so that the price on the computer screen when placing the order may not be the price when the order is filled.

To protect themselves, some online investors place **limit orders** stating the maximum price they are willing to pay or, if selling, the minimum price they're willing to take. A limit order may not be filled at all if the stock's price is moving quickly.

Online trading brought millions of people into the markets for the first time. Until the mid-1970s, the only way to purchase securities was through so-called full service brokers who offered investing advice and sometimes tried to sell the investment products sponsored by their companies. Most of them wouldn't accept really small trades, such as 25 shares, because they earned their living by taking a percentage of the value of the transaction and small ones just weren't worth it. In 1995 the Charles Schwab Company broke the domination of the full service brokers by opening a discount brokerage firm. Offering minimal advice or research, Schwab was able to lower the fees.

In the mid-1990s, online interactive communications hit the scene. Among the first commercial uses of the Internet was stock trading at a deep discount level. New companies such as E*Trade and Quick & Reilly were able to cut commissions even further than Schwab by offering only trading, no advice, and no human contact. Computers could do everything. Online trading took the country by storm in part because of the low cost, and in part because it coincided with the bull market in technology. By the year 2000, some 10 million people had Internet-based brokerage accounts with one of about 100 companies in the field.

The retail investor—a term for individual investors as opposed to mutual fund managers or pension fund managers—became a powerful force. A few went to the extreme of quitting jobs and becoming **day traders,** buying and selling numerous stocks in a single day. Eventually, many of the large brokerage houses that had criticized online trading offered it to customers in order to remain competitive. But, in the long run, there's no way the small individual investor can truly compete with the professional money managers.

The Internet improved access to research and information for ordinary investors. Information that once took weeks to gather could suddenly be obtained in minutes. Announcements by large publicly traded companies once open only to professional stock analysts became available to all via Internet webcasts. Other websites allowed rapid comparisons of financial information about many different companies. Still others provided articles and commentary on investments previously available only through expensive newsletters. The Internet, still in its infancy, is already an indispensable tool for investors and for the financial services industry.

The opportunities for young people, as well as working men and women, to begin planning their financial future have never been greater. This book has tried to bring you the basic information and knowledge to build on as you start to chart your own course to financial security and prosperity. Good luck.

Appreciation—an increase in value

Asset allocation—investing your money according to your goals and how much risk you want to take

Bond—a note, like an IOU, issued by a company or government that has borrowed money, promising to repay the loan on a set date and to pay interest in the meantime.

Capital—another term for money

Certificate of Deposit (CD)—a document issued by a financial institution for a special account, held for a specified amount of time, that pays a higher rate of interest than a regular savings account

Common stock—a security representing ownership of part of a company

Compounding—a process by which a sum of money increases in value as interest is paid on it and it is reinvested

Contract—an agreement, enforceable in a court of law, that binds one party to do something with or for another

Day trader—one who buys and sells many stocks in a single day on a regular basis, usually clearing the books at the end of each day

Diversifying—putting your money into different types of investments to reduce risk

Dividends—shares of profits that are paid by companies to stockholders

Equities—another term for stocks or shares

Federal Deposit Insurance Corporation (FDIC)—a government agency that guarantees you won't lose your money—up to $100,000—if it's deposited in and FDIC-insured bank and that bank goes out of business

Futures—something (such as corn or soybeans) bought for future acceptance or sold for future delivery; futures may also be bought as a hedge against price changes

Inflation—any series of events that results in the prices of things going up, reducing the buying power or value of money

Initial Public Offering (IPO)—the first sale of new shares of stock

Limit Order—an instruction to buy or sell at a specific price

Liquidity—the ability to easily buy and sell something

Mutual fund—a pooling of money put in by many investors who pay a professional manager to invest it for them

New York Stock Exchange (NYSE)—an organization providing a place for investors' orders to be filled, and rules to govern trading activity

Options—things for which the right to buy or sell during a specific time period has been acquired

Principal—an amount of money invested or loaned

Rate of return—the gain or loss from an investment stated as a percentage of that amount

Retirement plan—a plan enabling people to invest money for their retirement, offering some tax advantages

Securities—another term for kinds of investments, such as common stocks and bonds

Securities & Exchange Commission (SEC)—a United States government agency that oversees and regulates the investment industry

Securities Investor Protection Corporation (SIPC)—a group that protects investors from brokerage fraud

Shares—portions of ownership in a company

Speculator—one who buys and sells stocks hoping for quick gains

Stocks—shares of businesses that are sold to investors

Stock exchange or stock market—a place where orders to buy and sell stocks are brought together and filled by brokers acting as agents for the public

Bamford. Janet. *Street Wise: A Guide for Teen Investors.* Princeton, New Jersey: Bloomberg Press, 2000.

Edelman, Ric. *The Truth About Money.* New York: Harper Resource, 2000.

Hagstrom, Robert G. *The Warren Buffett Way: Investment Strategies of the World's Greatest Investor.* New York: John Wiley & Sons, 1997.

Modu, Emmanuel, and Andrea Walker. *Teenvestor.Com: The Practical Investment Guide for Teens and Their Parents.* Newark, New Jersey: Gateway, 2000.

Smith, Pat, and Lynn Roney. *Wow the Dow: The Complete Guide to Teaching Your Kids How to Invest in the Stock Market.* New York: Simon & Schuster, 2000.

Tyson, Eric. *Investing For Dummies.* St. Paul, Minnesota: Hungry Minds, Inc., 1999.

page

2: Associated Press/Wide World Photos
6: Associated Press/Wide World Photos
8: Choptank Syndicate
11: Associated Press/Wide World Photos
14: Library of Congress
17: Choptank Syndicate
19: Library of Congress
20: Associated Press/Wide World Photos
24: Associated Press/Wide World Photos
27: Library of Congress
30: Associated Press/Wide World Photos

32: Associated Press/Wide World Photos
36: Library of Congress
38. Choptank Syndicate
42: Associated Press/Wide World Photos
45: Associated Press/Wide World Photos
46: Associated Press/Wide World Photos
48: Associated Press/Wide World Photos
50: Associated Press/Wide World Photos
53: Courtesy of Otter Tail Corporation
56: Courtesy of Royce & Associates, Inc.

FRED BARBASH is a Washington writer. He retired from *The Washington Post* in July 2001 after 25 years at the paper, most recently as the paper's investing columnist and business editor. He has served as *The Post*'s National Editor, Chief of the London Bureau, and U.S. Supreme Court correspondent. He is the author of *The Founding: A Dramatic Account of the Writing of the Constitution*, Simon and Schuster, 1987.